Healing Shawls

When words are not enough, a healing shawl gives comfort, support, and love to those facing challenging times. This book shares patterns and ideas for how to create and give these meaningful gifts, as well as personal stories of giving that helped loved ones take comfort in a time of need. The 15 crochet designs are created with beloved Lion Brand® yarns (see page 48 for details). Whether you choose colors that are serene or vibrant, the soft yarns will help your gifts deliver a heartfelt message!

About Lion Brand® Yarn Company

Lion Brand® Yarn Company is a 5th generation, family-owned and operated business, and a beloved American brand since 1878. The company is devoted to inspiring and educating knitters and crocheters with yarns, patterns, how-tos, and ideas that elevate their yarn crafting experience.

LEISURE ARTS, INC. • Maumelle, Arkansas

ACKNOWLEDGMENTS

Lion Brand® Yarn Company and Leisure Arts would like to thank the many individuals who so graciously gave of their time in our research and shared with us their stories of inspiration and compassion.

LION BRAND® PRODUCTION TEAM
Vice President, Marketing: Ilana Rabinowitz
Production Manager: Ceresa Newsome
Creative Director: Adina Klein
Technical Editor: Jackie Smyth
Design Editor: Susan Haviland
Design Associate: Faye Rubenstein

LEISURE ARTS EDITORIAL STAFF
Senior Product Director: Pam Stebbins
Creative Art Director: Katherine Laughlin
Special Projects Director: Susan Frantz Wiles
Technical Writer: Lois J. Long
Art Category Manager: Lora Puls
Graphic Artist: Cailen Cochran
Prepress Technician: Stephanie Johnson
Contributing Photographer: Jason Masters
Contributing Photo Stylist: Lori Wenger

LEISURE ARTS BUSINESS STAFF
President and Chief Executive Officer: Fred F. Pruss
Senior Vice President of Operations: Jim Dittrich
Vice President of Retail Sales: Martha Adams
Chief Financial Officer: Tiffany P. Childers
Controller: Teresa Eby
Information Technology Director: Brian Roden
Director of E-Commerce: Mark Hawkins
Manager of E-Commerce: Robert Young

ISBN-13/EAN: 978-1-4647-3630-8
UPC: 0-28906-06500-8

Making Shawls of Comfort

for Physical and Emotional Healing

Introduction

There are occasions in life when it seems difficult to know what you can say or do that can make a difference. For those times when words can't fully convey your support, caring, and concern, crochet provides a way to let someone know how you feel.

A comfort shawl tells someone that you have thought of them throughout the hours-long process of crocheting a gift by hand. A comfort shawl tells someone that you have given of yourself—your time, your energy, and your loving care—to create something for them that doesn't exist anywhere else in the world.

A comfort shawl is a way to give someone a warm hug that can bring healing into their life. When it wraps around their shoulders, they can feel the loving hand that created it.

Occasions

There are many situations in which you might want to give a comfort shawl. Some examples are the loss of a loved one or serious illness of a loved one, the diagnosis of a serious illness, or a personal or financial setback in life, such as divorce or the loss of a job.

There are also positive and precious times when a life transition calls for something more than a gift from a department store. These include marriage, graduation, becoming a parent or grandparent, welcoming someone new into the family, or going away to college.

What Makes a Comfort Shawl Different

Do you own anything that was given to you by someone important in your life, or have an heirloom that was handed down from a family member who passed? When you wear this item or see it in a special place in your home, do you get a feeling that it is totally different from anything else you own? Would you ever consider parting with this gift if it became worn or no longer looked fresh? There is an energy that can live on in the things people create and the small, special treasures that they have held dear. Those material possessions have meaning and create feelings beyond their price.

Putting your thoughts and feelings into a handmade gift can have the same power to pass those positive, hopeful, and warm feelings to others. When you crochet a comfort shawl, you will be thinking about the recipient much of the time. You might meditate or simply say certain words to yourself over and over again. These thoughts will comfort you and will be conveyed to the person who wears it.

As you crochet, consider the qualities of the person who needs support. Say them to yourself. Silently repeat simple wishes for peace, comfort, and strength. Even without words, as you enjoy the meditative qualities of the stitching, have an image of the person in mind as you experience positive feelings for him or her.

Inspiration for Your Shawl

To get ideas for creating and giving shawls, look throughout this book for personal stories that were shared on the Lion Brand® blog. These touching tales demonstrate how the process of making and presenting shawls has benefited those who stitched them as well as those who received the finished gifts. If you would like to read more about the healing powers of knitting and crochet, visit the Lion Brand® blog archive and check out the category called "Wellness." You'll find it at blog.lionbrand.com.

Chevron Shawl

EASY

SIZE

About 24" x 54" (61 cm x 137 cm)

SHOPPING LIST

Yarn (Medium Weight) MEDIUM 4

LION BRAND® HEARTLAND®
(Art. #136)

☐ #105 Glacier Bay - 5 balls
or color of your choice

Crochet Hook

LION BRAND® crochet hook

☐ Size J-10 (6 mm)
or size needed for gauge

Additional Supplies

☐ LION BRAND® large-eyed blunt needle

GAUGE

1 ripple = about 4½" (11.5 cm) measured from peak to peak.

8 rows = about 4" (10 cm) in ripple pattern.

BE SURE TO CHECK YOUR GAUGE.

STITCH GUIDE

DOUBLE CROCHET 2 TOGETHER (abbreviated dc2tog)

(Yarn over, insert hook in next st and draw up a loop, yarn over and draw through 2 loops) twice, yarn over and draw through all 3 loops on hook – 1 st decreased.

DOUBLE CROCHET 3 TOGETHER (abbreviated dc3tog)

(Yarn over, insert hook in next st and draw up a loop, yarn over, draw through 2 loops) 3 times, yarn over and draw through all 4 loops on hook – 2 sts decreased.

DOUBLE CROCHET 4 TOGETHER (abbreviated dc4tog)

(Yarn over, insert hook in next st and draw up a loop, yarn over, draw through 2 loops) 4 times, yarn over and draw through all 5 loops on hook – 3 sts decreased.

NOTES

1. Shawl is worked in a ripple crochet pattern. The ripple pattern is easy to do, but it's important to remember that you may need to work several rows before the ripple pattern becomes clear.
2. The ripple in this design is created by skipping sts on sc rows and working dctogs on dc rows to form 'valleys' and working (sc, ch 2, sc) on sc rows and (dc, ch 3, dc) on dc rows to form 'peaks'. Take care to work valleys centered over valleys and peaks into the ch-sp of peaks of previous row.
3. An edging is worked across both short edges.

SHAWL

Ch 241.

Row 1 (RS): Sc in 2nd ch from hook and in next 9 ch, *ch 2, sc in next 9 ch, sk next 2 ch, sc in next 9 ch; rep from * to last 10 ch, ch 2, sc in last 10 ch – you will have 218 sc and 12 ch-2 sps forming 12 ripples at the end of this row.

Row 2: Ch 3 (does not count as st), turn, sk first st, dc2tog, (ch 1, sk next st, dc in next st) 3 times, ch 1, sk next st, (dc, ch 3, dc) in next ch-2 sp, dc in next 7 sts, *dc4tog, (ch 1, sk next st, dc in next st) 3 times, ch 1, sk next st, (dc, ch 3, dc) in next ch-2 sp, dc in next 7 sts; rep from * to last 3 sts, dc3tog – 144 dc and 12 ch-3 sps.

Row 3: Ch 1, turn, sc in first 9 sts, (sc, ch 2, sc) in next ch-3 sp, (sc in next st, sc in next ch-1 sp) 4 times, *sk next st, sc in next 8 sts, (sc, ch 2, sc) in next ch-3 sp, (sc in next st, sc in next ch-1 sp) 4 times; rep from * to last dc2tog, sk dc2tog, sc in top of turning ch.

Rows 4-7: Rep Rows 2 and 3 twice.

Row 8: Ch 3 (does not count as st), turn, sk first st, dc2tog, dc in next 7 sts, (dc, ch 3, dc) in next ch-2 sp, (ch 1, sk next st, dc in next st) 3 times, *ch 1, sk next st, dc4tog, dc in next 7 sts, (dc, ch 3, dc) in next ch-2 sp, (ch 1, sk next st, dc in next st) 3 times; rep from * to last 4 sts, ch 1, sk next st, dc3tog.

Row 9: Ch 1, turn, sc in first st, (sc in next ch-1 sp, sc in next st) 4 times, (sc, ch 2, sc) in next ch-3 sp, sc in next 8 sts, *sk next st, (sc in next ch-1 sp, sc in next st) 4 times, (sc, ch 2, sc) in next ch-3 sp, sc in next 8 sts; rep from * to last dc2tog, sk dc2tog, sc in top of turning ch.

Rows 10-13: Rep Rows 8 and 9 twice.

Rows 14-49: Rep Rows 2-13 three times.

Fasten off.

FINISHING

Edging

From RS, join yarn with a sl st in corner to work across a short edge of Shawl.

Row 1 (RS): Ch 1, working in ends of rows, work sc evenly spaced across short edge.

Fasten off.

Rep edging across other end of Shawl.

Weave in ends.

Comfort for a Care-Giver

My friend Bonnie has been an absolute rock and comfort to her husband of +28 years as he has battled cancer. We had worked together for 3 years, and it was going to be very hard for us not to see each other every day. I wanted to give her something more meaningful than the usual cursory gift.

I knew it was the perfect gift for her. I don't remember the yarn, just that it was blues I think -- and Bonnie loves the calming effect of being at the sea.

I have made many afghans and shawls and given them as gifts to family members and friends. This was, by far, the most meaningful and emotional gift I have ever made.

I stopped at the end of every row to think about Bonnie and what she was, and still is, going through and thought of her with love in every stitch. It was without a doubt the most important item I have ever created.

It was an emotional day made even more so when she opened her gift. She uses it often and tells me she always feels as though I am giving her a warm, comforting hug.

A Caring Friend

Openwork Cape Shawl

EASY +

Shown on page 9.

SIZE

Finished Circumference at neck:

About 26½" (67.5 cm), untied

Finished Circumference at lower edge: About 72" (183 cm)

Finished Length:

About 13½" (34.5 cm)

SHOPPING LIST

Yarn (Medium Weight) MEDIUM 4

LION BRAND® VANNA'S CHOICE® (Art. #860)

☐ #107 Sapphire - 3 balls

or color of your choice

Crochet Hook

LION BRAND® crochet hook

☐ Size J-10 (6 mm)

or size needed for gauge

Additional Supplies

☐ LION BRAND® large-eyed blunt needle

GAUGE

5 pattern reps = about 3" (7.5 cm).

Note: One pattern rep consists of one st (dc or sc) and the following ch-1 sp of Rows 1 and 2.

BE SURE TO CHECK YOUR GAUGE.

NOTES

1. Shawl is worked back and forth in rows, beginning at neck.
2. To shape shawl, shorter ch-sps are worked between sts near neck edge and longer ch-sps are worked between sts near lower edge.

SHAWL

Ch 92.

Row 1 (RS): Working in back bars of foundation ch, dc in 6th ch from hook (5 skipped ch count as 1 base ch, first dc, and first ch-1 sp), *ch 1, sk next ch, dc in next ch; rep from * across – you will have 45 dc and 44 ch-1 sps at the end of this row.

Row 2: Ch 1, turn, sc in first dc, *ch 1, sk next ch-1 sp, sc in next dc; rep from * to turning ch-sp, ch 1, sk next ch of turning ch, sc in next ch of turning ch – 45 sc and 44 ch-1 sps.

Row 3: Ch 1, turn, (sc, ch 2, sc) in first sc, *sk next ch-1 sp, (sc, ch 2, sc) in next sc; rep from * across – 90 sc and 45 ch-2 sps.

Rows 4-7: Ch 1, turn, (sc, ch 2, sc) in each ch-2 sp across.

Rows 8-13: Ch 1, turn, (sc, ch 2, sc) in first ch-2 sp, *ch 1, (sc, ch 2, sc) in next ch-2 sp; rep from * across – 90 sc, 45 ch-2 sps, and 44 ch-1 sps.

Rows 14-19: Ch 1, turn, (sc, ch 2, sc) in first ch-2 sp, *ch 2, (sc, ch 2, sc) in next ch-2 sp; rep from * across – 90 sc and 89 ch-2 sps.

Row 20: Ch 1, turn, (sc, ch 2, sc) in first ch-2 sp, *ch 3, sk next ch-2 sp, (sc, ch 2, sc) in next ch-2 sp; rep from * across – 90 sc, 45 ch-2 sps, and 44 ch-3 sps.

Rows 21-26: Ch 1, turn, (sc, ch 2, sc) in first ch-2 sp, *ch 3, sk next ch-3 sp, (sc, ch 2, sc) in next ch-2 sp; rep from * across – 90 sc, 45 ch-2 sps, and 44 ch-3 sps.

Row 27: Ch 1, turn, (sc, ch 2, sc) in first ch-2 sp, *ch 4, sk next ch-3 sp, (sc, ch 2, sc) in next ch-2 sp; rep from * across – 90 sc, 45 ch-2 sps, and 44 ch-4 sps.

Rows 28-30: Ch 1, turn, (sc, ch 2, sc) in first ch-2 sp, *ch 4, sk next ch-4 sp, (sc, ch 2, sc) in next ch-2 sp; rep from * across – 90 sc, 45 ch-2 sps, and 44 ch-4 sps.

Border (RS): Turn, sl st in first ch-2 sp, ch 3 (counts as dc), (dc, ch 2, 2 dc) in same ch-2 sp, ch 1, sl st in next ch-4 sp, *ch 1, (2 dc, ch 2, 2 dc) in next ch-2 sp, ch 1, sl st in next ch-4 sp; rep from * to last ch-2 sp, ch 1, (2 dc, ch 2, dc, ch 3, sl st) in last ch-2 sp; working in ends of rows across edge, (ch 3, sk end of next row, sl st in end of next row) 14 times, ch 3; working across opposite side of foundation ch, (sl st, ch 3, sl st) in ch at base of first dc, **ch 2, sk next ch, sl st in ch at base of next dc; rep from ** to turning ch-sp, ch 2, sk next ch, (sl st, ch 3, sl st) in next ch; working in ends of rows across edge, ch 3, sl st in end of Row 2, (ch 3, sk next row, sl st in end of next row) 14 times.

Fasten off.

TIE

With 2 strands of yarn held together and leaving a 6" (15 cm) long beginning yarn tail, make a chain about 76" (193 cm) long.

Fasten off, leaving a 6" (15 cm) long ending yarn tail.

Weave chain through sps between sts at neck of Shawl.

Tassel

Cut three 12" (30.5 cm) long strands of yarn. Hold strands together and knot at center of one end of chain – you'll have 8 strands of yarn extending from end of chain. Trim yarn ends to about 2" (5 cm).

Rep on opposite end of chain.

FINISHING

Weave in ends.

Everyday Eyelet Shawl

EASY +

SIZE

Finished Width:

About 70" (178 cm), across top edge

Finished Length:

About 35" (89 cm), not including edging

SHOPPING LIST

Yarn (Medium Weight) MEDIUM 4

LION BRAND® VANNA'S CHOICE® (Art. #860)

☐ #300 Denim Mist - 6 balls **or** color of your choice

Crochet Hook

LION BRAND® crochet hook

☐ Size K-10½ (6.5 mm) **or** size needed for gauge

Additional Supplies

☐ LION BRAND® large-eyed blunt needle

GAUGE

11 dc = about 4" (10 cm).

BE SURE TO CHECK YOUR GAUGE.

NOTES

1. Shawl is worked in one piece with increases worked at one edge only for shaping. The increase edge becomes the top edge of the Shawl.
2. Edging is worked around outside edge of Shawl.

SHAWL

Ch 2.

Row 1 (RS): Work 2 sc in 2nd ch from hook – 2 sc.

Row 2: Ch 4 (does not count as a st), turn, 2 dc in first st, dc in last st – you will have 3 dc at the end of this row.

Row 3: Ch 1, turn, sc in each st to turning ch-sp, 2 sc in turning ch-sp – 5 sc.

Row 4: Ch 4 (does not count as a st), turn, 2 dc in first st, dc in each st across – 6 dc.

Row 5: Rep Row 3 – 8 sc.

Row 6 (Mesh Row): Ch 6 (does not count as a st), turn, sk first st, dc in next st, *ch 2, sk next 2 sts, dc in next st; rep from * across – 3 dc, 2 ch-2 sps and 1 turning ch-sp.

Row 7: Ch 1, turn, sc in each dc and ch to turning ch-sp, sc in first 2 ch of turning ch, 2 sc in turning ch-sp – 11 sc.

Row 8: Rep Row 4 – 12 dc.

Rows 9 and 10: Rep Rows 3 and 4 – 15 dc.

Row 11: Rep Row 3 – 17 sc.

A Gift for Hospitalized Mom

I made a comfort shawl for my mom when she went into the hospital for exploratory surgery. I thought a shawl would keep her warm in the hospital and let her know I'm thinking of her. I made it with 4 skeins of Lion Brand Homespun in the color Delft. My mom appreciated the love that went into the shawl and kept it with her in the hospital. It comforted me to know she had part of me near her even when I wasn't there.

Andrea G.

Rows 12-89: Rep Rows 6-11 thirteen more times – you will have 134 sts at the end of Row 89.

Do not fasten off.

Top Edging

Row 1 (RS): Rotate piece to work in ends of rows across long side edge (top edge of Shawl), ch 2 (does not count as a st), work 1 hdc in end of each sc row, 3 hdc in end of each dc row, 4 hdc in end of each mesh row, and 1 hdc in edge of foundation row.

Row 2: Ch 2 (does not count as a st), turn, 2 hdc in first st, hdc in each st to last st, 2 hdc in last hdc.

Row 3: Ch 1, turn, 2 sc in first st, sc in each st to last st, 2 sc in last st.

Do not fasten off.

Bottom Edging

Row 1 (RS): Rotate piece to work in ends of rows across next side edge, ch 1, sc in end of each of the 3 top edging rows; working in ends of rows across Shawl edge, work 1 sc in foundation ch at base of first sc, work 1 sc in end of each sc row, 2 sc in end of each dc row, and 2 sc in end of each mesh row to corner (for a total of 134 sc worked evenly across Shawl edge plus 3 sc worked in ends of top edging rows), 3 sc in corner (lower point); working in sts of next edge, sc in each st across to top edging row, work sc in end of each of the 3 top edging rows – 277 sc (137 sts on each side of 3-sc corner).

Row 2: Ch 1, turn, 2 sc in first st, sc in each st to center sc of 3-sc corner, 3 sc in center st, sc in each st to last st, 2 sc in last st – 281 sc (139 sts on each side of 3-sc corner).

Row 3: Ch 1, turn, sc in first st, ch 3, sk next 3 sts, *sc in next st, ch 3, sk next 3 sts; rep from * to center sc of 3-sc corner, (sc, ch 3, sc) in center st, **ch 3, sk next 3 sts, sc in next st; rep from ** to end of row – 72 sc and 71 ch-3 sps (35 ch-3 sps on each side of corner ch-3 sp).

Row 4: Turn, sl st in first st, (sl st, ch 1, 3 sc) in next ch-3 sp, ch 1, *3 sc in next ch-3 sp, ch 1; rep from * to corner ch-3 sp, 5 sc in corner ch-3 sp, **ch 1, 3 sc in next ch-3 sp; rep from ** to end of row – 215 sc (Thirty-five 3-sc groups on each side of corner 5-sc group) and 70 ch-1 sps.

Row 5: Turn, sl st in first st, ch 1, sc in next st (center st of first 3-sc group), *ch 2, (2 dc, ch 6, sl st in 5th ch from hook, ch 1, 2 dc) in center st of next 3-sc group, ch 2, sc in next center st of next 3-sc group; rep from * to corner 5-sc group, (3 dc, ch 6, sl st in 5th ch from hook, ch 1, 3 dc) in center st of 5-sc corner, ch 2, sc in center st of next 3-sc group, **ch 2, (2 dc, ch 6, sl st in 5th ch from hook, ch 1, 2 dc) in center st of next 3-sc group, ch 2, sc in center st of next 3-sc group; rep from ** to end of row, sl st in last st.

Fasten off.

FINISHING

Weave in ends.

Multidirectional Shawl

EASY +

Shown on page 15.

SIZE

Finished Width at lower edge: About 32" (81.5 cm)

Finished Width at top edge: About 62" (157.5 cm)

Finished Length: About 26" (66 cm)

SHOPPING LIST

Yarn (Bulky Weight) BULKY 5

LION BRAND® UNIQUE®
(Art. #755)

- ☐ #205 Grapevine - 8 balls
  or color of your choice

Crochet Hook

LION BRAND® crochet hook

- ☐ K-10½ (6.5 mm)
  or size needed for gauge

Additional Supplies

- ☐ LION BRAND® large-eyed blunt needle

GAUGE

11 hdc + 8 rows = about 4" (10 cm).
BE SURE TO CHECK YOUR GAUGE.

STITCH GUIDE

HALF DOUBLE CROCHET 2 TOGETHER (abbreviated hdc2tog)

(Yarn over, insert hook in next st and draw up a loop) twice, yarn over and draw through all 5 loops on hook – 1 st decreased.

HALF DOUBLE CROCHET 3 TOGETHER (abbreviated hdc3tog)

(Yarn over, insert hook in next st and draw up a loop) 3 times, yarn over and draw through all 7 loops on hook – 2 sts decreased.

NOTES

1. Shawl is made from 3 Triangles. Triangles II and III are worked across edges of the previous Triangle.
2. A border is worked around the outside edge of Shawl.

TRIANGLE I

Ch 84.

Row 1 (RS): Sc in 2nd ch from hook and in each sc across – 83 sc.

Row 2: Ch 2 (counts as first hdc in this row and in all following rows), turn, hdc in next st and in each st across.

Row 3 (Decrease Row): Ch 2, turn, hdc2tog; working in back loops only, hdc in each st to last 3 sts, hdc2tog; working in both loops, hdc in last st (top of turning ch) – 81 sts.

Row 4 (Decrease Row): Ch 2, turn, hdc2tog, hdc in each st to last 3 sts, hdc2tog, hdc in last st – 79 sts.

Row 5 (Decrease Row): Rep Row 3 – 77 sts.

Row 6: Ch 3 (counts as hdc, ch 1), turn, sk next st, hdc in next st, *ch 1, sk next st, hdc in next st; rep from * across – 39 hdc and 38 ch-1 sps.

Rows 7-50: Rep Rows 3-6 eleven more times – 6 hdc and 5 ch-1 sps at the end of Row 50.

Note: When repeating Row 3, each hdc and ch-1 sp of the previous row counts as a st.

Rows 51-53: Rep Rows 3-5 – 5 sts.

Row 54: Ch 2, turn, hdc in next st and in each st across.

Row 55: Ch 2, turn, hdc3tog, hdc in last st – 3 sts.

Row 56: Ch 1, turn, sk first 2 sts, sc in top of turning ch – 1 st.

Fasten off.

TRIANGLE II

Row 1 (RS): From RS and following diagram, join yarn with a sl st in lower corner of Triangle I to work across one side edge, ch 1, work 83 sc evenly spaced across side edge.

Note: To work 83 sc evenly across the edge, you can work as follows: Work 8 sc evenly spaced across edges of Rows 1-5, (work 6 sc across edges of next 4 rows) 11 times, work 9 sc across edges of Rows 50-56.

Rows 2-56: Work same as Rows 2-56 of Triangle I.

Fasten off.

TRIANGLE III

Row 1 (RS): From RS and following diagram, join yarn with a sl st in lower corner of Triangle II to work across one side edge, ch 1, work 83 sc evenly spaced across side edge.

Rows 2-56: Work same as Rows 2-56 of Triangle I.

Do not fasten off.

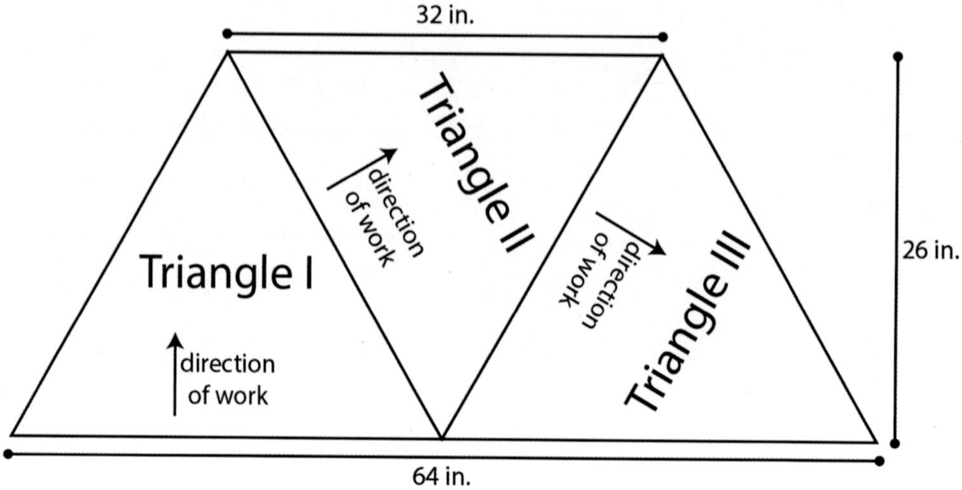

FINISHING

Border

Rnd 1 (RS): Ch 1, turn, work 82 sc evenly spaced across each side edge of each Triangle, working 2 sc in each join between Triangles and 3 sc in each point.

Rnd 2: Turn, working in front loops only, sl st in each st around.

Fasten off.

Weave in ends.

When I'm Gone

I made each of my children and grandchildren a shawl for when I'm no longer on this earth and they will have my thoughts and prayers for them to hug and know I love them so much.

I used their favorite colors and a very soft, cuddly yarn.

I was very touched while making them and made lapghans for the boys. I wrote them each a letter and gave them a piece of the yarn. They cried when they read the note and were very touched.

I felt good inside. My children and grandchildren told me that the shawl is kept on their bed so that when they need it, it's close by.

Leaving a Legacy

Mantra Shawl

EASY

SIZE

About 20" x 65" (51 cm x 165 cm), including borders

SHOPPING LIST

Yarn (Bulky Weight) BULKY 5

LION BRAND® UNIQUE®
(Art. #755)

- ☐ #203 Passion Fruit - 6 balls
  or color of your choice

Crochet Hook

LION BRAND® crochet hook

- ☐ Size N-13 (9 mm)
  or size needed for gauge

Additional Supplies

- ☐ LION BRAND® large-eyed blunt needle

GAUGE

2 V-sts = about 4" (10 cm).
BE SURE TO CHECK YOUR GAUGE.

STITCH GUIDE

V-STITCH (abbreviated V-st)
(Dc, ch 1, dc) in indicated st or sp.

SHELL
Work 11 dc in indicated st.

NOTE

Shawl is worked in one piece in an easy V-st pattern.

SHAWL

Ch 42.

Set-Up Row: Sc in 2nd ch from hook, *ch 5, sk next 3 ch, sc in next ch; rep from * across – you will have 10 ch-5 sps at the end of this row.

Row 1 (RS): Ch 3 (counts as first dc), turn, dc in first sc, *ch 1, sc in next ch-5 sp, ch 1, V-st in next sc; rep from * to last ch-5 sp, ch 1, sc in last ch-5 sp, ch 1, 2 dc in last sc – 9 V-sts.

Row 2: Ch 1, turn, sc in first dc, *ch 5, sk next 2 ch-1 sps, sc in ch-1 sp of next V-st; rep from * to last 2 ch-1 sps, ch 5, sk last 2 ch-1 sps, sc in top of turning ch.

Rep Rows 1 and 2 until piece measures about 60" (152.5 cm) from beg, end with a Row 1 as the last row you work.

Next Row (WS): Ch 1, turn, sc in first dc, ch 3, sk first 2 ch-1 sps, sc in ch-1 sp of next V-st, *ch 3, sk next 2 ch-1 sps, sc in ch-1 sp of next V-st; rep from * to last 2 ch-1 sps, ch 3, sk last 2 ch-1 sps, sc in top of turning ch.

Do not fasten off.

Top Border Row (RS): Ch 1, turn, sc in first sc, *sk next ch-3 sp, shell in next sc, sk next ch-3 sp, sc in next sc; rep from * across – 5 shells.

Fasten off.

Lower Border Row (RS): From RS, working across opposite side of foundation ch, join yarn with sc in ch at base of first sc, *sk next 3 ch, shell in ch at base of next sc, sk next 3 ch, sc in ch at base of next sc; rep from * across – 5 shells.

Fasten off.

FINISHING

Weave in ends.

A Hug Across the Ocean

I reconnected with my cousin Patricia when I traveled back to my hometown outside of Philadelphia in the summer of 2013. Shortly after my return to my new home in Northern Ireland, I found out that she was ill and would require surgery. I couldn't visit her or run errands for her, but I wanted her to know that I was thinking of her and that I deeply cared. My lacy shawl was the way I found to do that.

I kept track of Patricia's illness and recovery through Facebook posts from her daughter and, when she was feeling up to it, from Patricia herself. Each night after work, I'd check for messages and knit a few more rows, thinking of her and wishing her wellness with each stitch.

Patricia was touched that I had taken my time and talents and created something just for her. She read my note that explained why I wanted to give her this shawl and she burst into tears, hugging the shawl. I felt loved and appreciated, but more importantly, I felt grateful that I was able to make her feel loved.

A Loving Cousin

Lacy V-Stitch Shawl

EASY

SIZE

About 24" x 70" (61 cm x 178 cm)

SHOPPING LIST

Yarn (Super Bulky Weight) SUPER BULKY 6

LION BRAND® HOMESPUN® THICK & QUICK® (Art. #792)

☐ #315 Tudor - 3 skeins
or color of your choice

Crochet Hook

LION BRAND® crochet hook

☐ Size P-15 (10 mm)
or size needed for gauge

Additional Supplies

☐ LION BRAND® large-eyed blunt needle

GAUGE

2 pattern reps = about 4" (10 cm).

Note: One pattern rep consists of one V-st and the following ch-2 sp.
BE SURE TO CHECK YOUR GAUGE.

STITCH GUIDE

V-STITCH (abbreviated V-st)

(Sc, ch 3, sc) in indicated st or sp.

NOTES

1. Shawl is worked in 2 halves.
2. The first half is worked back and forth in rows beg at center back, then the second half is worked across the opposite side of the foundation ch.
3. First and second halves are identical.

SHAWL

First Half

Ch 35.

Row 1 (RS): V-st in 2nd ch from hook, *ch 2, skip next 2 ch, V-st in next ch; rep from * across – you will have 12 V-sts and 11 ch-2 sps at the end of this row.

Row 2: Ch 1, turn, V-st in ch-3 sp of first V-st, *ch 2, V-st in ch-3 sp of next V-st; rep from * across.

Rep Row 2 until piece measures about 35" (89 cm) from beg.

Fasten off.

Second Half

Row 1 (RS): From RS, working across opposite side of foundation ch, join yarn with sc in ch at base of first V-st, ch 3, sc in same ch as joining (first V-st made), *ch 2, V-st in ch at base of next V-st; rep from * across – you will have 12 V-sts and 11 ch-2 sps at the end of this row.

Healing a Relationship

She was my ex-mother-in-law and at age 90 her heart was failing. The doctors tried a pacemaker, but her heart was simply giving up and she was in hospice care.

I sent the shawl along to her via one of my children, as she tired easily and only immediate family was allowed. When she opened it, she was surprised and stunned that I would make it for her. She called me on the phone to thank me.

My relationship with my former mother-in-law was rocky at best and sometimes extremely difficult. In some ways we were too much alike and in some ways too opposite, in all the wrong ways. When she called to thank me for the shawl, we had a chance for some real healing between us, and I am grateful we had that opportunity because she passed away about 6 weeks later. It was more than worth the time and effort to have that bad feeling gone.

Grateful

Row 2: Ch 1, turn, V-st in ch-3 sp of first V-st, *ch 2, V-st in ch-3 sp of next V-st; rep from * across.

Rep Row 2 until second half measures about 35" (89 cm).

Note: Entire piece should measure about 70" (178 cm).

Fasten off.

FINISHING

Weave in ends.

Gentle Waves Shawl

EASY

SIZE

About 20" x 62" (51 cm x 157.5 cm)

SHOPPING LIST

Yarn (Bulky Weight) BULKY 5

LION BRAND® HOMESPUN® (Art. #790)

- ☐ #418 Ambrosia - 1 skein (A)
- ☐ #426 Tulips - 1 skein (B)
- ☐ #411 Mixed Berries - 1 skein (C)

or colors of your choice

Crochet Hook

LION BRAND® crochet hook

- ☐ Size K-10½ (6.5 mm)

or size needed for gauge

Additional Supplies

- ☐ LION BRAND® large-eyed blunt needle

GAUGE

3 blocks = about 5½" (14 cm);
5 rows = about 4¼" (11 cm).
BE SURE TO CHECK YOUR GAUGE.

NOTES

1. Shawl is worked back and forth in rows.
2. Edging is worked across both ends.
3. To change yarn color, work last st of old color to last yarn over. Yarn over with new color and draw through all loops on hook to complete st. Proceed with new color. Do not cut old color. Carry colors not in use up side of the piece until next needed.

SHAWL

With A, ch 232.

Row 1: Work 2 dc in 4th ch from hook (first 3 ch count as dc), sk next 3 ch, sc in next ch, *ch 3, dc in next 3 ch, sk next 3 ch, sc in next ch; rep from * across – you will have 32 ch-3 sps, and 33 sc at the end of this row.
Change to B.

Row 2: With B, ch 3 (counts as first dc), turn, 2 dc in first sc, *sk next 3 dc, (sc, ch 3, 2 dc) in next ch-3 sp, dc in next sc; rep from * across, sc in top of turning ch.
Change to C.

Row 3: With C, rep Row 2.
Change to A.

Row 4: With A, rep Row 2.
Change to B.

Rows 5-22: Rep Rows 2-4.
Change to B.

Rows 23 and 24: Rep Rows 2 and 3. Do not change to A at the end of Row 24.

Cut A and B. Continue with C only.

First Side Edging

Row 1 (RS): Working in ends of rows across side edge, ch 1, (sc, ch 3, 3 dc) in end of last row, *sk next row, (sc, ch 3, 3 dc) in end of next row; rep from * across edge, sc in corner.

Fasten off.

Second Side Edging

From RS, join C with sl st in end of first row at beg of other side edge, ch 1, (sc, ch 3, 3 dc) in end of same row, *sk next row, (sc, ch 3, 3 dc) in end of next row; rep from * across edge, sc in corner.

Fasten off.

FINISHING

Weave in ends.

Paneled Shawl

EASY +

SIZE

About 20" x 60" (51 cm x 152.5 cm)

SHOPPING LIST

Yarn (Medium Weight) MEDIUM 4

LION BRAND® VANNA'S CHOICE® (Art. #860)

- ☐ #405 Silver Heather - 3 balls (A)
- ☐ #123 Beige - 1 ball (B)
- ☐ #135 Rust - 1 ball (C)
- ☐ #133 Brick - 1 ball (D)

  or colors of your choice

Crochet Hook

LION BRAND® crochet hook

- ☐ Size J-10 (6 mm)

  or size needed for gauge

Additional Supplies

- ☐ LION BRAND® large-eyed blunt needle

GAUGE

2 pattern reps = about 4" (10 cm) across Center Panel.

Note: One pattern rep consists of one V-st + the following Shell.
BE SURE TO CHECK YOUR GAUGE.

STITCH GUIDE

REVERSE SINGLE CROCHET (abbreviated rev sc)

Single crochet worked from left to right (right to left, if left-handed). Insert hook into next stitch to the right (left), under loop on hook, and draw up a loop. Yarn over, draw through all loops on hook.

SHELL

(2 hdc, ch 1, 2 hdc) in indicated st or sp.

V-STITCH (abbreviated V-st)

(Hdc, ch 1, hdc) in indicated st or sp.

NOTES

1. Center Panel is worked first, then Side Panels are worked on each end of Center Panel.
2. A border is worked around the outside edge of the Shawl.
3. To change yarn color, work last st of old color to last yarn over. Yarn over with new color and draw through all loops on hook to complete the st. Proceed with new color. Fasten off old color.

SHAWL

Center Panel

With A, ch 48.

Row 1: V-st in 4th ch from hook (3 skipped ch count as 1 foundation ch and first hdc), *sk next 2 ch, Shell in next ch, sk next 2 ch, V-st in next ch; rep from * to last 2 ch, sk next ch, hdc in last ch – at the end of Row 1 you will have 8 V-sts, 7 Shells, and 2 hdc (one at each end of row).

Row 2: Ch 2 (counts as hdc), turn, Shell in ch-1 sp of first V-st, *V-st in ch-1 sp of next Shell, Shell in ch-1 sp of next V-st; rep from * across, hdc in top of turning ch – 7 V-sts, 8 Shells, and 2 hdc.

Row 3: Ch 2 (counts as hdc), turn, V-st in ch-1 sp of first Shell, *Shell in ch-1 sp of next V-st, V-st in ch-1 sp of next Shell; rep from * across, hdc in top of turning ch – 8 V-sts, 7 Shells, and 2 hdc.

Rep Rows 2 and 3 until piece measures about 40" (101.5 cm) from beg.
Change to B.

First Side Panel

Row 1 (RS): With B, ch 4 (counts as dc, ch 1), turn, 3 dc in first ch-1 sp, *ch 1, 3 dc in next ch-1 sp; rep from * across, ch 1, dc in top of turning ch – Fifteen 3-dc groups, 16 ch-1 sps, and 2 dc.

Row 2: With B, ch 3 (counts as dc), turn, dc in first st, sk first ch-1 sp, *ch 1, 3 dc in next ch-1 sp; rep from * across, ch 1, 2 dc in 3rd ch of turning ch – Fourteen 3-dc groups, 15 ch-1 sps, and 4 dc (one 2-dc group at each end of row).
Change to C.

Row 3: With C, ch 4 (counts as dc, ch 1), turn, 3 dc in first ch-1 sp, *ch 1, 3 dc in next ch-1 sp; rep from * to last 2 dc, ch 1, sk next dc, dc in top of turning ch – Fifteen 3-dc groups, 16 ch-1 sps, and 2 dc.

Row 4: With C, rep Row 2.
Change to B.

Rows 5 and 6: With B, rep Rows 3 and 4.
Change to C.

Rows 7 and 8: With C, rep Rows 3 and 4.
Change to D.

Rows 9 and 10: With D, rep Rows 3 and 4.
Change to C.

Rows 11 and 12: With C, rep Rows 3 and 4.

Fasten off.

Second Side Panel

From RS, working across opposite side of foundation ch, join B with sl st in ch at base of first hdc.

Row 1 (RS): With B, ch 4 (counts as dc, ch 1), 3 dc in ch at base of next V-st, *ch 1, 3 dc in ch at base of next Shell, ch 1, 3 dc in ch at base of next V-st; rep from * across, ch 1, dc in last ch – 15 V-sts, 16 ch-1 sps, and 2 dc.

Rows 2-12: Work same as Rows 2-12 of first side panel.
Change to B.

Border

Rnd 1 (RS): Ch 3 (counts as dc), turn, 2 dc in first ch-sp, *ch 1, 3 dc in next ch-1 sp; rep from * across, ch 1, (3 dc, ch 2, 3 dc) in turning ch-sp for corner; working in ends of rows across long edge, **ch 1, sk next row, 3 dc in end of next row; rep from ** across edge, ch 1; working in sts along short edge, (3 dc, ch 2, 3 dc) in first ch-1 sp for corner, ***ch 1, 3 dc in next ch-1 sp; rep from *** to last ch-sp, ch 1, (3 dc, ch 2, 3 dc) in last ch-sp for corner; working in ends of rows across long edge, ****ch 1, sk next row, 3 dc in end of next row; rep from **** across edge, ch 1, 3 dc in last ch-sp, ch 2; join with sl st in top of beg ch.

Fasten off.

Rnd 2: From RS, join C with sl st in any ch-1 sp, ch 3 (counts as dc), 2 dc in same ch-1 sp, *ch 1, 3 dc in next ch-1 sp; rep from * around, working (3 dc, ch 2, 3 dc) in each corner ch-2 sp; join with sl st in top of beg ch.

Fasten off.

Rnd 3: With D, rep Rnd 2.

Do not fasten off.

Rnd 4: With D, ch 1, skipping the ch-1 sps, work rev sc in each dc and corner ch-2 sp around; join with sl st in beg ch.

Fasten off.

FINISHING

Weave in ends.

A Reminder of Hope

I felt my friend needed a shawl because he had been recovering from a nasty concussion, and anyone who has had one or knows someone who had one knows that they can be serious and cause all kinds of problems. My friend was having a lot of trouble with depression and negative thoughts of hurting himself and others, and it scared him to death. I reached out to him and we talked, and I told him that if he ever needed someone, he could call me; and I got the idea to make him a shawl for those times when he couldn't contact me or needed to know that he wasn't alone and hadn't been abandoned.

I started and restarted over a dozen times, wanting it to be just right; but knowing my friend, he wouldn't care if it wasn't, so I kept my thoughts on him and I thought about what he had told me and what we talked about together, and I was amazed myself that I could finish it in 6 hours. He cried a little when I gave it to him, and he hugged me so tight and thanked me for being there for him when he was so sure everyone else had abandoned him. I hugged him back and told him nothing he could do would make me leave, that I would always stick by him even if nobody else would. I've given shawls before, but I have never had a reaction like this one and I'll always remember it. My friend is doing better, and whenever I see the shawl in his car I remember the day I gave it to him and it makes me smile.

Jeannie P.

Serene Shells Shawl

EASY +

SIZE

About 20" x 64" (51 cm x 162.5 cm)

SHOPPING LIST

Yarn (Bulky Weight) BULKY 5

LION BRAND® HOMESPUN® (Art. #790)

- ☐ #341 Windsor - 2 skeins (A)
- ☐ #315 Tudor - 1 skein (B)
- ☐ #329 Waterfall - 1 skein (C)

or colors of your choice

Crochet Hook

LION BRAND® crochet hook

- ☐ Size K-10½ (6.5 mm)

or size needed for gauge

Additional Supplies

- ☐ LION BRAND® large-eyed blunt needle

GAUGE

2 shells = about 4½" (11.5 cm);
6 rows = about 4" (10 cm).
BE SURE TO CHECK YOUR GAUGE.

STITCH GUIDE

SHELL

(3 dc, ch 1, 3 dc) in indicated st or sp.

NOTES

1. Shawl is worked in 2 halves. First half is worked in rows, beginning at center. Sts of the second half are worked across the first half.
2. To change yarn color, work last st of old color to last yarn over. Yarn over with new color and draw through all loops on hook to complete the st. Proceed with new color. Fasten off old color.

SHAWL

First Half

With A, ch 164.

Row 1 (RS): Sc in 2nd ch from hook, *sk next 2 ch, Shell in next ch, sk next 2 ch, sc in next ch; rep from * to end of row – you will have 28 sc and 27 Shells at the end of this row.
Change to B.

Row 2: Ch 5 (counts as dc, ch 2), turn, sc in ch-1 sp of first Shell, ch 2, dc in next sc, *ch 2, sc in ch-1 sp of next Shell, ch 2, dc in next sc; rep from * to end of row – 28 dc, 27 sc, and 54 ch-2 sps.

Row 3: Ch 3 (counts as first dc in this row and in all following rows), turn, 2 dc in first dc, sk next ch-2 sp, sc in next sc, *sk next ch-2 sp, Shell in next dc, sk next ch-2 sp, sc in next sc; rep from * to turning ch-sp, 3 dc in 3rd ch of turning ch – 27 sc, 26 Shells, and one 3-dc group at beg and end of row.
Change to A.

To Honor Military Service

The shawl I made was a gift to be sent overseas to an unknown, actively serving military member. I believe that our soldiers overseas need constant reminders that they are not alone and that back home we appreciate their efforts. The shawl was like a hug the soldier could wear whenever needed. Since this shawl was shipped in a care package with many other items, and nothing more special than my name on the tag attached to the shawl, when I got an unexpected "thank-you" card from the soldier who received the shawl, I was overwhelmed. The female soldier told me in her "thank-you" note that she believed the shawl would make her stronger and thus help her to better support the soldiers in her medical care. Knowing that I could make that small difference made me want to do more to help our military personnel.

Janelle S.

Row 4: Ch 1, turn, sc in first dc, ch 2, dc in next sc, *ch 2, sc in ch-1 sp of next Shell, ch 2, dc in next sc; rep from * to last 3-dc group, ch 2, sc in top of turning ch – 28 sc, 27 dc, and 54 ch-2 sps.

Row 5: Ch 1, turn, sc in first sc, *sk next ch-2 sp, Shell in next dc, sk next ch-2 sp, sc in next sc; rep from * across.
Change to C.

Rows 6 and 7: With C, rep Rows 2 and 3.
Change to A.

Rows 8 and 9: With A, rep Rows 4 and 5.
Change to B.

Rows 10 and 11: With B, rep Rows 2 and 3.
Change to C.

Rows 12 and 13: With C, rep Rows 4 and 5.
Change to A.

Rows 14 and 15: With A, rep Rows 2 and 3.

Fasten off.

Second Half

Row 1 (RS): From RS and working across opposite side of foundation ch, join A with sc in ch at base of first sc, *sk next 2 ch, Shell in ch at base of next Shell, sk next 2 ch, sc in ch at base of next sc; rep from * across.
Change to B.

Rows 2-15: Work same as Rows 2-15 of First Half.

Do not fasten off.

Note: Edging is worked in ends of rows across both side edges. Each side edging is worked in the same way as Row 3 of the Shawl as follows: 3 dc are worked in beg corner, then sc are alternated with Shells to work 7 Shells evenly spaced across, ending with 3 dc in opposite corner.

First Side Edging (RS): Continuing with A, 3 dc in same ch as last 3-dc group made, do not turn, working in ends of rows across side edge of Second Half, sc in end of Row 14, *sk next row, Shell in end of next row, sk next row, sc in end of next row; rep from * 2 more times, Shell in end of Row 1; working in ends of rows across side edge of First Half, sk Row 1, sc in end of next row, **sk next row, Shell in end of next row, sk next row, sc in end of next row; rep from ** 2 more times, 3 dc in same ch as 3-dc group at end of Row 15 – 8 sc, 7 Shells, and one 3-dc group at beg and end.

Fasten off.

Second Side Edging (RS): From RS, join A with a sl st in same dc as first 3-dc group of Row 15 of first half, ch 3, 2 dc in same dc, complete edging same as first side edging.

Fasten off.

FINISHING

Weave in ends.

Simple Shells Shawl

EASY

Shown on page 31.

SIZE

About 14½" x 63½" (37 cm x 161.5 cm)

SHOPPING LIST

Yarn (Medium Weight) MEDIUM 4

LION BRAND® VANNA'S CHOICE® (Art. #860)

- ☐ #143 Antique Rose - 4 balls **or** color of your choice

Crochet Hook

LION BRAND® crochet hook

- ☐ Size J-10 (6 mm) **or** size needed for gauge

Additional Supplies

- ☐ LION BRAND® large-eyed blunt needle

GAUGE

2 pattern reps = about 3½" (9 cm); 7½ rows = about 4" (10 cm).

Note: One pattern rep consists of one Shell and the following sc of the RS rows.

BE SURE TO CHECK YOUR GAUGE.

STITCH GUIDE

SHELL

Work 5 dc in indicated st.

NOTES

1. Shawl is worked in two identical halves. Sts are worked into the opposite side of the foundation ch of first half to beg second half.
2. A border is worked all the way around the outer edge of Shawl.

SHAWL

First Half

Ch 50.

Row 1 (RS): Working in back bars of ch, sc in 2nd ch from hook, *sk next 2 ch, Shell in next ch, sk next 2 ch, sc in next ch; rep from * across – you will have 8 Shells and 9 sc at the end of this row.

Row 2: Ch 3 (counts as first dc in this row and in all following rows), turn, dc in first sc, ch 2, sc in center dc of next Shell, *ch 2, dc in next sc, ch 2, sc in center dc of next Shell; rep from * to last sc, ch 2, 2 dc in last sc – 8 sc, 11 dc, and 16 ch-2 sps.

Row 3: Ch 1, turn, sk first dc, sc in next dc, *Shell in next sc, sc in next dc; rep from * across; leave turning ch unworked – 8 Shells and 9 sc.

Rows 4-59: Rep Rows 2 and 3.

Fasten off.

Second Half

Row 1 (RS): From RS and working across opposite side of foundation ch, join yarn with sc in ch at base of first sc, *Shell in ch at base of next Shell, sc in ch at base of next sc; rep from * across – 8 Shells and 9 sc.

Rows 2-59: Work same as Rows 2-59 of first half.

Fasten off.

FINISHING

Border

From RS, draw up a loop of yarn in center of either long side (at edge of foundation ch), ch 1, ****(sc, ch 3, sc) in same sp; working across long edge, sc in side of sc at end of first row, *ch 5, sk next row, sl st in side of sc at end of next row; rep from * to last 2 rows, ch 5, sk next row, (sl st, ch 3, sl st) in side of sc at end of last row for corner; working across sts of last row, **ch 3, (sl st, ch 3, sl st) in center dc of next Shell, ch 3, sl st in next sc; rep

Remembering a Teacher

I heard that a favorite teacher from high school had been in a bad car accident and would be hospitalized for a few weeks, at least. While I mused what I could send him (I'm no longer living in that area), he suffered a stroke as a result of surgery. So, not only was his body broken, but he had some brain damage as well.

I thought the pattern was properly masculine, but I wanted it to be as soft and comfortable as possible, with minimum weight and a colorway for a man. Homespun fit the bill on all counts; being "easy care" was a great plus, too. The original pattern made a stole, but I increased the dimensions for more coverage as a bed jacket. In addition, I hoped it would be useful as a wheelchair blanket.

When I visited, I don't think he recognized me specifically, but he was really happy that a former student was visiting. He didn't make much of the gift while I was there. He had to focus on chatting (his speech was slurred). But, later I was surprised to receive a letter from his son which told me that he loves the blanket and won't get in his wheelchair without knowing that it's right there to go on his lap, even going outdoors in warm weather. When I read that, I was so touched. I was also motivated to make a Cotton-Ease blanket in summery colors, so that he wouldn't be overheated.

A nurse actually went out of his way to stop me and ask if I was a charity knitter, and if I would make others for the indigent men on his ward. He said, of all the donated knitting, men only occasionally received caps meant for chemo caps, or rarely a lap blanket meant for layettes (usually too small for adults). But that blanket was the first handmade donation he'd ever seen intentionally made for a man.

Jenna

from ** 6 more times, ch 3, (sl st, ch 3, sl st) in center dc of last Shell, ch 3, (sl st, ch 3, sl st) in last sc for corner; working across side edge, ***ch 5, sk next row, sl st in side of sc at end of next row; rep from *** to last 2 rows before foundation ch, ch 5, sk next row, sc in side of sc at end of first row; rep from **** once more; join with sl st in first sc.

Fasten off.

Weave in ends.

Retreat Shawl

EASY +

SIZE

Finished Width:

About 54" (137 cm) measured along top edge, not including edging

Finished Length:

About 24" (61 cm) at center

SHOPPING LIST

Yarn (Super Bulky Weight) SUPER BULKY 6

LION BRAND® HOMESPUN® THICK & QUICK® (Art. #792)

☐ #211 Granite Stripes - 3 skeins or color of your choice

Crochet Hook

LION BRAND® crochet hook

☐ Size P-15 (10 mm) or size needed for gauge

Additional Supplies

☐ LION BRAND® stitch markers

☐ LION BRAND® large-eyed blunt needle

GAUGE

1 pattern rep = about 3" (7.5 cm); 2 rows = about 3½" (9 cm) in Rows 1-10 of Shawl.

Note: One pattern rep consists of one 3-dc group and the following ch-1 sp.

BE SURE TO CHECK YOUR GAUGE.

NOTES

1. Shawl is worked back and forth in rows in a 'Granny Stitch' pattern of 3-dc groups worked into sps of previous row.
2. A 3-dc group is added at the beg and end of each row, and two 3-dc groups are skipped at center of each row. This means that each row will have the same number of 3-dc groups. Increasing and decreasing in this manner shapes the Shawl.
3. Edging is worked along the 2 short side edges and lower edge.

SHAWL

Ch 76.

Row 1: Work 3 dc in 5th ch from hook (4 skipped ch count as first dc, ch 1), (ch 1, sk next 3 ch, 3 dc in next ch) 8 times, (do not ch 1), sk next 5 ch, 3 dc in next ch, place a marker in the sp between last two 3-dc groups made, (ch 1, sk next 3 ch, 3 dc in next ch) 8 times, ch 1, dc in last ch – you will have eighteen 3-dc groups at the end of this row.

Rows 2-11: Ch 4 (counts as dc, ch 1), turn, 3 dc in first ch-1 sp, *ch 1, 3 dc in next ch-1 sp; rep from * to marker, (do not ch 1), sk marked sp, 3 dc in next ch-1 sp, move marker to sp between last two 3-dc groups made, **ch 1, 3 dc in next ch 1-sp; rep from ** to turning ch-sp, ch 1, (3 dc, ch 1, dc) in turning ch-sp.

Do not fasten off.

Edging

Place 9 markers along each short edge, placing the first marker at one corner, the 2nd marker at the opposite corner and the 7 remaining markers as evenly spaced as possible between the first 2 markers.

Row 1: Ch 5 (counts as tr, ch 1), do not turn, working across short edge, (tr, ch 2, tr) at first corner marker, *ch 1, (tr, ch 2, tr) at next marker, remove marker; rep from * to next corner marker, ch 1, (tr, ch 2, tr, ch 2, tr, ch 2, tr) at corner marker, place a marker in the center ch-2 sp of the 3 ch-2 corner sps just made; working across opposite side of foundation ch, **ch 1, (tr, ch 2, tr) in ch at base of next 3-dc group; rep from ** to center ch-5 sp, ch 1, (tr, ch 2, tr, ch 2, tr, ch 2, tr) in center ch of ch-5 sp, place a marker in the center ch-2 sp of the 3 ch-2 corner sps just made, ***ch 1, (tr, ch 2, tr) in ch at base of next 3-dc group; rep from *** to next corner marker, ch 1, (tr, ch 2, tr, ch 2, tr, ch 2, tr) at corner marker, place a marker in the center ch-2 sp of the 3 ch-2 corner sps just made, ****ch 1, (tr, ch 2, tr) at next marker, remove marker; rep from **** to next corner marker, (tr, ch 2, tr, ch 1, tr) at corner marker.

Note: When this row is complete, you should only have markers remaining in the center ch-2 sps at the 3 lower corners.

Row 2: Ch 5 (counts as tr, ch 1), turn, 3 dc in first ch-1 sp, *working into the ch-2 sps only (skipping the ch-1 sps), (ch 1, 3 dc in next ch-2 sp) to marked corner ch-2 sp, ch 2, (2 dc, tr, 2 dc) in marked corner ch-2 sp and move marker to center tr just made, ch 2, 3 dc in next ch-2 sp; rep from * twice more, skipping the ch-1 sps, (ch 1, 3 dc in next ch-2 sp) to turning ch-sp, ch 1, (3 dc, ch 1, tr) in turning ch-sp.

Row 3: Ch 5 (counts as tr, ch 1), turn, 3 dc in first ch-1 sp, *(ch 1, 3 dc in next ch-sp) to marked corner tr, ch 1, (2 dc, tr, 2 dc) in corner tr and move marker to center tr just made; rep from * twice more, (ch 1, 3 dc in next ch-sp) to turning ch-sp, ch 1, (3 dc, ch 1, tr) in turning ch-sp.

Row 4: Ch 1, turn, *sc in each st and ch-sp to marked corner tr, 3 sc in corner tr, remove marker; rep from * twice more, sc in each st and ch-sp to end of row.

Fasten off.

FINISHING

Weave in ends.

Giving Warmth to a Loved One

My step-grandmother was 97 years old and in good health. She was a resident at the Pioneer Manor Nursing Home and was always feeling a chill.

I made her a comfort shawl for her shoulders and a lap blanket for her lap.

I used a very soft pink wool, since this was a favorite color of hers, and I did it in a single crochet so that it would be a tight stitch to keep in the warmth. When she received the shawl and lap blanket, Alice was very, very happy. She used them for the next 10 years. Alice was kept warm by my gift of love until she passed away, one day shy of her 107th birthday.

Monique B.

Small Squares Shawl

EASY

Shown on page 37.

SIZE

About 21" x 60" (53.5 cm x 152.5 cm), not including border

SHOPPING LIST

Yarn (Medium Weight) 4

LION BRAND® VANNA'S CHOICE® (Art. #860)

☐ #108 Dusty Blue - 3 balls (A)

LION BRAND® VANNA'S PALETTES (Art. #865)

☐ #200 Peaceful - 2 packages (B)

☐ #205 Essential - 2 packages (C)

or colors of your choice

Crochet Hook

LION BRAND® crochet hook

☐ Size J-10 (6 mm)

or size needed for gauge

Additional Supplies

☐ LION BRAND® large-eyed blunt needle

GAUGE

One Square = about 3" x 3" (7.5 cm x 7.5 cm).

BE SURE TO CHECK YOUR GAUGE.

NOTES

1. Shawl is made from 140 Squares: 5 Squares worked with each color of B and C for a total of 80 Squares and 60 Squares worked with A.
2. Squares are crocheted tog following a diagram.
3. Border is worked around entire outer edge of assembled Shawl.

SQUARES (make 140 – 60 with A and 5 with each color of B and C)

Ch 4; join with sl st in first ch to form a ring.

Rnd 1 (RS): Ch 3 (counts as first dc), 2 dc in ring, (ch 1, 3 dc in ring) 3 times, ch 1; join with sl st in top of beg ch – Four 3-dc groups and 4 ch-1 sps.

Rnd 2: Sl st in next 2 dc, sl st in first ch-1 sp, ch 3 (counts as first dc), (3 dc, ch 1, 4 dc) in same ch-1 sp (first corner made), *(4 dc, ch 1, 4 dc) in next ch-1 sp (corner made); rep from * 2 more times; join with sl st in top of beg ch – Eight 4-dc groups and 4 corner ch-1 sps.

Fasten off.

ASSEMBLY

From RS, arrange Squares into a rectangle of 20 rows of 7 Squares each, as shown in diagram on page 36. B and C Squares should be placed as desired.

Crochet the corners of neighboring Squares tog. When joining Squares along the edges of the Shawl follow the "Join 2 Corners" instructions. For all other Squares, follow the "Join 4 Corners" instructions. All Squares are joined tog using A.

Join 2 Corners: From RS, join A with a sl st in corner of first Square, ch 1, yarn over, insert hook into corresponding corner of neighboring Square and draw up a loop (3 loops on hook), yarn over and draw through all loops on hook, ch 1, sl st in beg ch-1.

Fasten off.

Tie securely and weave in ends.

Join 4 Corners: From RS, join A with a sl st in corner of first Square, *ch 1, yarn over, insert hook into corresponding corner of next neighboring Square and draw up a loop (3 loops on hook), yarn over and draw through all loops on hook; rep from * 2 more times, ch 1, sl st in beg ch-1.

Fasten off.

Tie securely and weave in ends.

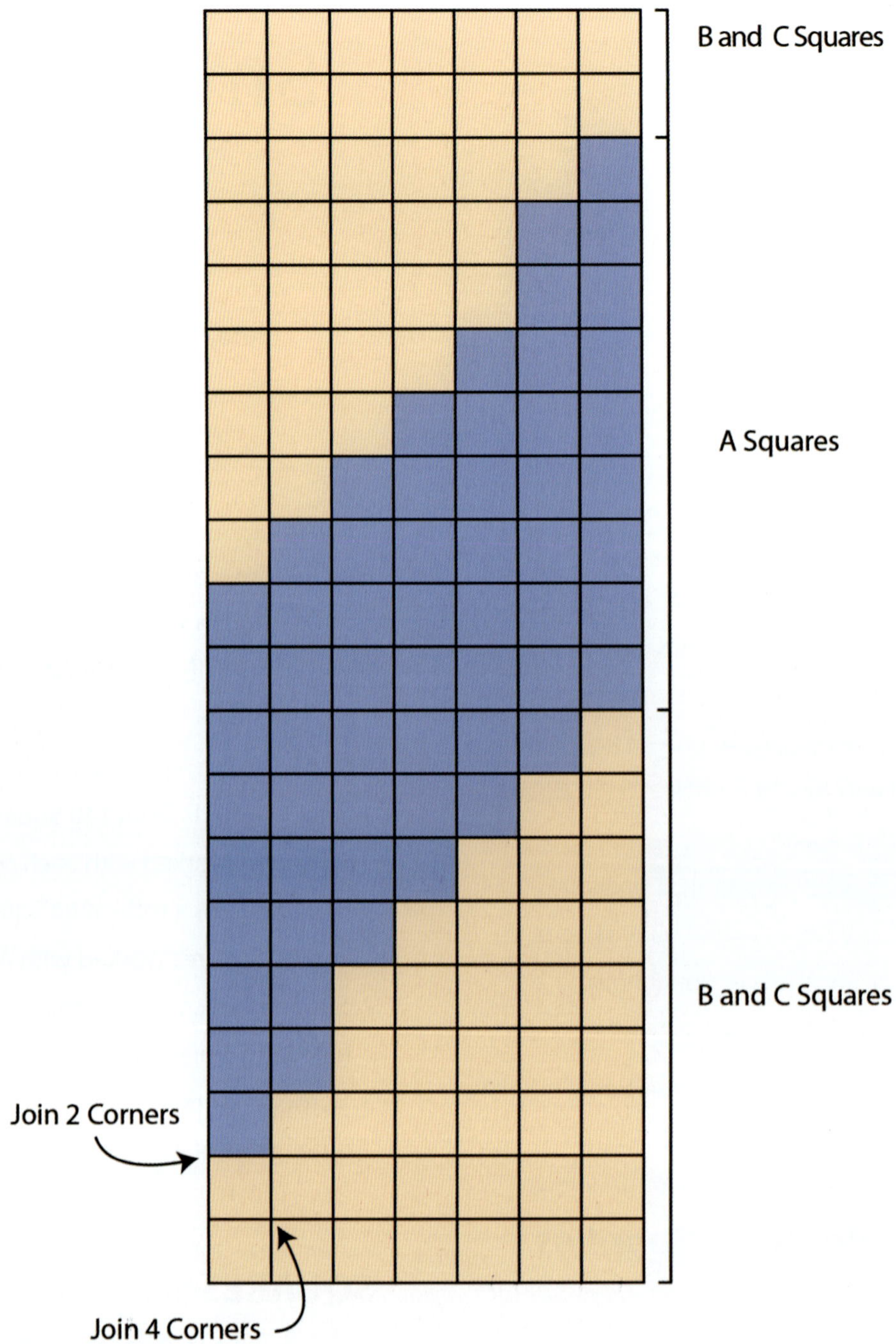

FINISHING

Border

From RS, join A with sl st in sp between 4-dc groups on side of any Square, *ch 5, sc in join between Squares, ch 5, (sc, ch 5, sl st) in next sp between 4-dc groups; rep from * around, working (sc, ch 5, sl st) in each corner; join with sl st in same sp as first sl st.

Fasten off.

Weave in ends.

Learning What a Gift Means

A relative's spouse had a pituitary gland tumor, and I wanted to show her that I cared. I thought the shawl would be like giving her a much needed hug.

I made the shawl with Homespun in a light blue variegated color. My pattern was simple. I used size 13 needles and cast on 69 stitches. I knit one row and then knit 3, purl 3 on the next row. I used 3 skeins of Homespun.

My aunt found a poem to go with the shawl to the recipient. Since we felt we would cry while reading it, we asked her husband to read it -- and he cried! I make numerous shawls for cancer patients so I don't usually know the outcome, but with the experience I described here, I can only imagine the comfort it gives to anyone that receives it.

Anonymous Giver

Soft Shades Shawl

EASY +

SIZE

About 24" x 54" (61 cm x 137 cm)

SHOPPING LIST

Yarn (Super Bulky Weight) SUPER BULKY 6

LION BRAND® HOMESPUN® THICK & QUICK® (Art. #792)

☐ #412 Pearls - 1 skein (A)

☐ #201 Coral Stripes - 2 skeins (B)

or colors of your choice

Crochet Hook

LION BRAND® crochet hook

☐ Size P-15 (10 mm)

or size needed for gauge

Additional Supplies

☐ LION BRAND® large-eyed blunt needle

GAUGE

6 dc = about 4" (10 cm).

BE SURE TO CHECK YOUR GAUGE.

NOTES

1. Shawl is worked in rows, changing yarn color every row.
2. To change yarn color, work last st of old color to last yarn over. Yarn over with new color and draw through all loops on hook to complete st.
3. When instructed to drop a loop from hook, enlarge the loop or place it on a stitch marker or safety pin to keep it from unraveling. When instructed to pick up a dropped loop, place the loop back onto the hook and gently tighten.

SHAWL

With A, ch 110.

Row 1 (RS): Sc in 2nd ch from hook, *ch 3, sk next 3 ch, sc in next ch; rep from * across – you will have 28 sc and 27 ch-3 sps at the end of this row. Change to B. Drop loop of A, but do not fasten off.

Row 2: With B, ch 3 (counts as first dc in this row and in all following rows), turn, 3 dc in each ch-3 sp across, dc in last sc – 83 dc (arranged in twenty-seven 3-dc groups and 1 dc at beg and end of row). Drop loop of B, but do not fasten off.

Row 3: Do not turn, return to beg of row just finished and insert hook in first ch (ch at base) of beg ch-3, yarn over with dropped loop of A and draw through, sl st in 2nd ch of beg ch, (sl st, ch 1, sc) in 3rd ch of beg ch, *ch 3, sk next 3-dc group, sc in next sp between 3-dc groups; rep from * to last 3-dc group, ch 3, sk last 3-dc group, insert hook in last dc and draw up a loop (2 loops on hook), pick up dropped loop of B (3 loops on hook) and draw through 2 loops on hook. Drop loop of A, but do not fasten off.

Rep Rows 2 and 3 until piece measures about 24" (61 cm) from beg; end with a Row 2 as the last row you work.

Next Row: With A, work same as Row 3 to last 3-dc group, ch 3, sk last 3-dc group, sc in last dc.

Fasten off B, but do not fasten off A.

Edging: With A and working in ends of rows across end of Shawl, work (ch 3, sk end of next B row, sc in end of next A row) across edge.

Fasten off.

Join A with sc to work across opposite end of Shawl and work edging across.

Fasten off.

FINISHING

Weave in ends.

Triangle Shawl

EASY +

SIZE

About 66" (167.5 cm) at widest x 33" (84 cm) long at center

SHOPPING LIST

Yarn (Bulky Weight) BULKY 5

LION BRAND® HOMESPUN®
(Art. #790)

☐ #315 Tudor - 2 skeins
or color of your choice

Crochet Hook

☐ Size L-11 (8 mm)
or size needed for gauge

Additional Supplies

☐ LION BRAND® stitch markers

☐ LION BRAND® large-eyed blunt needle

GAUGE

Rows 1-6 of Shawl = about 22" (56 cm) at widest x 11" (28 cm) long at center.

BE SURE TO CHECK YOUR GAUGE.

STITCH GUIDE

CENTER-FAN

(Tr, ch 1, dtr, ch 1, tr) in indicated st.

DOUBLE TREBLE/TRIPLE CROCHET (abrreviated dtr)

(Yarn over) 3 times, insert hook in indicated st and draw up a loop, (yarn over and draw through 2 loops on hook) 4 times.

FAN

(Tr, ch 1, tr, ch 1, tr) in indicated st or sp.

SHELL

5 tr in indicated st or sp.

V-STITCH (abbreviated V-st)

(Tr, ch 3, tr) in indicated st or sp.

NOTES

1. Shawl is worked in one piece with increases on each row for shaping.
2. Since this yarn is highly textured, markers are helpful in determining which st is which. Mark the center st of each Shell, Fan, or V-st as you work, then when you work the next row you will be able to see easily which sts to work into.

SHAWL

Ch 4.

Row 1: Sc in 2nd ch from hook and in each of rem 2 ch –3 sc.

Row 2: Ch 2 (counts as first hdc), turn, 2 hdc in first st, 3 hdc in rem 2 sts – at the end of this row you will have 9 hdc.

A Wish for a Mother and Baby

My friend Claire was diagnosed with breast cancer at the young age of 31 when she was pregnant with her first child. She opted not to undergo all the treatments, in order to give her son the best chance possible to survive and to be born without damage from the radiation and chemo. Claire said she wore that shawl to every doctor's appointment and would relate the story of its "birth" to all who were in the waiting rooms, as well as to the doctors and nurses caring for her. Her son, Dylan, was born squirming and squealing and is now nine years old. Claire's cancer went into remission and she is cancer free to this day. She will not have any more children but is thankful for her healthy son.

A Concerned Friend

Row 3: Ch 6 (counts as first dtr, ch 1 in this row and in all following rows), turn, sk first st, Shell in next st, ch 2, sk next 2 sts, dtr in next st (center), ch 2, sk next 2 sts, Shell in next st, ch 1, dtr in last st – 2 Shells, 4 ch-sps, and 3 dtr.

Row 4: Ch 6, turn, (Fan, tr) in first ch-sp, Fan in center st of next Shell, tr in next ch-sp, ch 2, Center-Fan in center dtr, ch 2, tr in next ch-sp, Fan in center st of next Shell, (tr, Fan, ch 1, dtr) in turning ch-sp – 5 Fans (4 regular Fans and 1 Center Fan).

Row 5: Ch 6, turn, (V-st, tr) in first ch-sp, (V-st in center st of next Fan, tr in next tr between Fans) twice, V-st in next tr, ch 2, dtr in center dtr, ch 2, V-st in next tr, (tr in next tr between Fans, V-st in center st of next Fan) twice, (tr, V-st, ch 1, dtr) in turning ch-sp – 8 V-sts.

Row 6: Ch 6, turn, tr in first st, tr in next ch-sp, *Fan in ch-sp of next V-st, tr in next tr between V-sts; rep from * to last V-st before center dtr, Fan in ch-sp of next V-st, tr in next ch-sp, ch 2, Center-Fan in center dtr, ch 2, tr in next ch-sp, Fan in ch-sp of next V-st, **tr in next tr between V-sts, Fan in ch-sp of next V-st; rep from ** to turning ch-sp, (2 tr, ch1, dtr) in turning ch-sp – 9 Fans (8 regular Fans and 1 Center Fan).

Row 7: Ch 6, turn, sk first ch-1 sp, Shell in next tr, tr in next tr, *Shell in center st of next Fan, tr in next tr between Fans; rep from * to ch-sp before Center Fan, sk next ch-sp, Shell in next tr, ch 2, dtr in center dtr, ch 2, Shell in next tr, **tr in next tr between Fans, Shell in center st of next Fan; rep from ** across, tr in next tr following last Fan, Shell in next tr, ch 1, dtr in turning ch-sp – 12 Shells.

Row 8: Ch 6, turn, tr in first st, tr in next ch-sp, *Fan in center st of next Shell, tr in next tr between Shells; rep from * to last Shell before center dtr, Fan in center st of next Shell, tr in next ch-sp, ch 2, Center-Fan in center dtr, ch 2, tr in next ch-sp, Fan in center st of next Shell, **tr in next tr between Shells, Fan in center st of next Shell; rep from ** to turning ch-sp, (2 tr, ch 1, dtr) in turning ch-sp – 13 Fans (12 regular Fans and 1 Center Fan).

Row 9: Ch 6, turn, sk first ch-1 sp, V-st in next tr, tr in next tr, *V-st in center st of next Fan, tr in next tr between Fans; rep from * to ch-sp before Center Fan, sk next ch-sp, V-st in next tr, ch 2, dtr in center dtr, ch 2, V-st in next tr, **tr in next tr between Fans, V-st in center st of next Fan; rep from ** across, tr in next tr following last Fan, V-st in next tr, ch 1, dtr in turning ch-sp – 16 V-sts.

Rows 10-15: Rep Rows 6-9 once, then rep Rows 6 and 7 once – 28 Shells at the end of Row 15.

Row 16: Ch 1, turn, sc in each st and ch-sp to center dtr, 3 sc in center dtr, sc in each st and ch-sp to end of row.

Fasten off.

FINISHING

Weave in ends.

Striated Triangles Shawl

EASY +

Shown on page 45.

SIZE

Finished Width at lower edge:

About 32" (81.5 cm)

Finished Width at top edge:

About 62" (157.5 cm)

Finished Length: About 26" (66 cm)

SHOPPING LIST

Yarn (Medium Weight) MEDIUM 4

LION BRAND® LANDSCAPES® (Art. #545)

☐ #204 Desert Spring - 6 balls **or** color of your choice

Crochet Hook

LION BRAND® crochet hook

☐ Size K-10.5 (6.5 mm) **or** size needed for gauge

Additional Supplies

☐ LION BRAND® large-eyed blunt needle

GAUGE

11 hdc + 8 rows = about 4" (10 cm).

BE SURE TO CHECK YOUR GAUGE.

STITCH GUIDE

HALF DOUBLE CROCHET 2 TOGETHER (abbreviated hdc2tog)

(Yarn over, insert hook in next st and draw up a loop) twice, yarn over and draw through all 5 loops on hook – 1 st decreased.

HALF DOUBLE CROCHET 3 TOGETHER (abbreviated hdc3tog)

(Yarn over, insert hook in next st and draw up a loop) 3 times, yarn over and draw through all 7 loops on hook – 2 sts decreased.

NOTES

1. Shawl is made from 3 Triangles. Triangles II and III are worked across edges of the previous Triangle.
2. A border is worked around the outside edge of Shawl.

TRIANGLE I

Ch 84.

Row 1 (RS): Sc in 2nd ch from hook and in each sc across – 83 sc.

Row 2: Ch 2 (counts as first hdc in this row and in all following rows), turn, hdc in next st and in each st across.

Row 3 (Decrease Row): Ch 2, turn, hdc2tog; working in back loops only, hdc in each st to last 3 sts, hdc2tog; working in both loops, hdc in last st (top of turning ch) – 81 sts.

Row 4 (Decrease Row): Ch 2, turn, hdc2tog, hdc in each st to last 3 sts, hdc2tog, hdc in last st – 79 sts.

Row 5 (Decrease Row): Rep Row 3 – 77 sts.

Row 6: Ch 3 (counts as hdc, ch 1), turn, sk next st, hdc in next st, *ch 1, sk next st, hdc in next st; rep from * across – 39 hdc and 38 ch-1 sps.

Rows 7-50: Rep Rows 3-6 eleven more times – 6 hdc and 5 ch-1 sps at the end of Row 50.

Note: When repeating Row 3, each hdc and ch-1 sp of the previous row counts as a st.

Rows 51-53: Rep Rows 3-5 – 5 sts.

Row 54: Ch 2, turn, hdc in next st and in each st across.

Row 55: Ch 2, turn, hdc3tog, hdc in last st – 3 sts.

Row 56: Ch 1, turn, sk first 2 sts, sc in top of turning ch – 1 st.

Fasten off.

TRIANGLE II

Row 1 (RS): From RS and following diagram, join yarn with a sl st in lower corner of Triangle I to work across one side edge, ch 1, work 83 sc evenly spaced across side edge.

Note: To work 83 sc evenly across the edge, you can work as follows: Work 8 sc evenly spaced across edges of Rows 1-5, (work 6 sc across edges of next 4 rows) 11 times, work 9 sc across edges of Rows 50-56.

Rows 2-56: Work same as Rows 2-56 of Triangle I.

Fasten off.

TRIANGLE III

Row 1 (RS): From RS and following diagram, join yarn with a sl st in lower corner of Triangle II to work across one side edge, ch 1, work 83 sc evenly spaced across side edge.

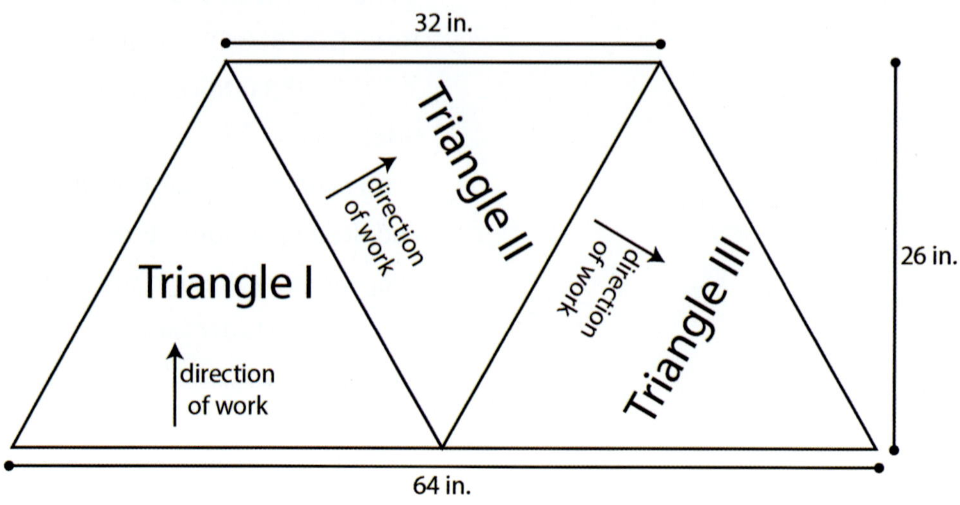

Rows 2-56: Work same as Rows 2-56 of Triangle I.

Do not fasten off.

FINISHING

Border

Rnd 1 (RS): Ch 1, turn, work 82 sc evenly spaced across each side edge of each Triangle, working 2 sc in each join between Triangles and 3 sc in each point.

Rnd 2: Turn, working in front loops only, sl st in each st around.

Fasten off.

Weave in ends.

A Friend Moves Away

Chris and I managed a group home together. Then she moved many states away. After she began her new work with Burmese refugees, she was diagnosed with Rheumatoid Arthritis. I thought the prayer shawl would be an encouragement to her and help her remember our friendship across the miles.

I used Homespun Gothic since purple is her favorite color. I used a triangle shawl pattern. Chris was surprised and delighted. Her joy made every dropped and corrected stitch worth it.

I like to keep my hands busy with projects that both challenge and relax me. But being able to give away the items I make gives me great joy.

Julanna K.

General Instructions

ABBREVIATIONS

beg = begin(ning)(s)
ch = chain
ch-sp(s) = chain space (s) previously made
cm = centimeter
dtr = double treble (triple) crochet
dc = double crochet
hdc = half double crochet
mm = millimeters
rem = remain(ing)(s)
rep (s) = repeat (s)
RS = right side
rnd(s) = round(s)
sc = single crochet
sk = skip
sl st = slip stitch
sp(s) = space(s)
st(s) = stitch(es)
tog = together
tr = treble (triple) crochet
WS = wrong side

* — When you see an asterisk used within a pattern row, the symbol indicates that later you will be told to repeat a portion of the instruction. Most often the instructions will say, repeat from * so many times.

( ) or **[ ]** — Sets off a short number of stitches that are repeated or indicates additional information.

— When you see – (dash) followed by a number of stitches, this tells you how many stitches you will have at the end of a row or round.

CROCHET TERMINOLOGY		
UNITED STATES		INTERNATIONAL
slip stitch (slip st)	=	single crochet (sc)
single crochet (sc)	=	double crochet (dc)
half double crochet (hdc)	=	half treble crochet (htr)
double crochet (dc)	=	treble crochet (tr)
treble crochet (tr)	=	double treble crochet (dtr)
double treble crochet (dtr)	=	triple treble crochet (ttr)
triple treble crochet (tr tr)	=	quadruple treble crochet (qtr)
skip	=	miss

GAUGE

Never underestimate the importance of gauge. Achieving the correct gauge assures that the finished size of your piece matches the finished size given in the pattern.

CHECKING YOUR GAUGE

Work a swatch that is at least 4" (10 cm) square. Use the suggested hook size and the number of stitches given. If your swatch is larger than 4" (10 cm), you need to work it again using a smaller hook; if it is smaller than 4" (10 cm), try it with a larger hook. This might require a swatch or two to get the exact gauge given in the pattern.

METRICS

As a handy reference, keep in mind that 1 ounce = approximately 28 grams and 1" = 2.5 centimeters.

TERMS

fasten off — To end your piece, you need to simply cut and pull the yarn through the last loop left on the hook. This keeps the last stitch intact and prevents the work from unraveling.

right side — Refers to the front of the piece.

Yarn Weight Symbol & Names	LACE 0	SUPER FINE 1	FINE 2	LIGHT 3	MEDIUM 4	BULKY 5	SUPER BULKY 6	JUMBO 7
Type of Yarns in Category	Fingering, size 10 crochet thread	Sock, Fingering, Baby	Sport, Baby	DK, Light Worsted	Worsted, Afghan, Aran	Chunky, Craft, Rug	Super Bulky, Roving	Jumbo, Roving
Crochet Gauge* Ranges in Single Crochet to 4" (10 cm)	32-42 sts**	21-32 sts	16-20 sts	12-17 sts	11-14 sts	8-11 sts	6-9 sts	5 sts and fewer
Advised Hook Size Range	Steel*** 6 to 8, Regular hook B-1	B-1 to E-4	E-4 to 7	7 to I-9	I-9 to K-10½	K-10½ to M/N-13	M/N-13 to Q	Q and larger

*GUIDELINES ONLY: The chart above reflects the most commonly used gauges and hook sizes for specific yarn categories.

** Lace weight yarns are usually crocheted with larger hooks to create lacy openwork patterns. Accordingly, a gauge range is difficult to determine. Always follow the gauge stated in your pattern.

*** Steel crochet hooks are sized differently from regular hooks–the higher the number, the smaller the hook, which is the reverse of regular hook sizing.

BEGINNER	Projects for first-time crocheters using basic stitches. Minimal shaping.
EASY	Projects using yarn with basic stitches, repetitive stitch patterns, simple color changes, and simple shaping and finishing.
INTERMEDIATE	Projects using a variety of techniques, such as basic lace patterns or color patterns, mid-level shaping and finishing.
EXPERIENCED	Projects with intricate stitch patterns, techniques and dimension, such as non-repeating patterns, multi-color techniques, fine threads, small hooks, detailed shaping and refined finishing.

CROCHET HOOKS																	
U.S.	B-1	C-2	D-3	E-4	F-5	G-6	7	H-8	I-9	J-10	K-10½	L-11	M/N-13	N/P-15	P/Q	Q	S
Metric - mm	2.25	2.75	3.25	3.5	3.75	4	4.5	5	5.5	6	6.5	8	9	10	15	16	19

YARN INFORMATION

The projects in this book were created with Lion Brand® yarns. For best results, we recommend following the pattern exactly as written. Be sure to purchase the amounts recommended in the pattern, and retain your labels. Always follow the care instructions provided on the label.

MEDIUM 4 **Heartland®**

Art. #136 available in solids (100% Acrylic), 5 oz (142 g), 251 yd (230 m) and tweeds (94% Acrylic, 6% Rayon), 4 oz (113 g), 200 yd (183 m) balls. **Made in the U.S.A.**

BULKY 5 **Unique®**

Art. #755 available in prismatic multicolors (100% Acrylic), 3.50 oz (100 g), 109 yd (100 m) balls.

MEDIUM 4 **Vanna's Palettes**

Art. #865 (100% Acrylic) available in package of 8 miniature skeins of complementary colors, 0.35 oz (10 g), 17 yd (16 m) skeins.

MEDIUM 4 **Landscapes®**

Art. #545 available in self-striping saturated colors and solids (100% Acrylic), 3.50 oz (100 g), 147 yd (134 m) balls.

BULKY 5 **Homespun®**

Art. #790 available in solids, heathers, and self-striping 'painterly' colors (98% Acrylic, 2% Polyester), 6 oz (170 g), 185 yd (169 m) balls. **Made in the U.S.A.**

VISIT LionBrand.com FOR:

- Learn to Knit & Crochet Instructions
- Weekly newsletter with articles, tips, and updates
- Store Locator

MEDIUM 4 **Vanna's Choice®**

Art. #860 (100% Premium Acrylic) available in solids, 3.50 oz (100 g), 170 yd (156 m), prints, tweeds, and heathers, 3 oz (85 g), 145 yd (133 m); and twists, 2.50 oz (70 g), 121 yd (111 m) balls.

SUPER BULKY 6 **Homespun® Thick & Quick®**

Art. #792 available in heathers and self-striping 'painterly' colors (88% Acrylic, 12% Polyester), 8 oz (227 g), 160 yd (146 m) balls. **Made in the U.S.A.**